Behaviour Management in the Early Years

by
Dr Hannah Mortimer

Published in 2006

© Hannah Mortimer

ISBN 978 1 898873 15 0

British Library Cataloguing
A catalogue record for this book is available from the British Library.

Published by QEd Publications, 39 Weeping Cross, Stafford ST17 0DG
Tel: 01785 620364
Website: www.qed.uk.com
Email: orders@qed.uk.com

Acknowledgement
Some of this material was first published as *Managing Children's behaviour* in 2004 by Scholastic.

Contents

Introduction

The aim of the book

This book gives you a framework for thinking about young children's behaviour and how to encourage children to behave appropriately if their behaviour becomes a problem. It will sit comfortably on your bookshelf with three other books by Hannah Mortimer from the same series – *Personal, Social and Emotional Development of Children in the Early Years* will give you an overview of how young children usually develop in this area; *Emotional Literacy and Mental Health in the Early Years* will help you identify children who might be at risk of emotional difficulties and suggests how you can support children who are emotionally vulnerable. Most importantly *An A-Z of Tricky Behaviours in the Early Years* forms a companion to the present book and provides you with specific information and guidance about particular behaviours. Whereas this book provides you with the general approaches that you need in order to manage behaviour in the early years, the 'A-Z' deals with specific behaviours such as biting, kicking or throwing temper tantrums.

Why have more than one book? This is because it is impossible to provide 'recipe book' approaches for 'solving' behaviours. Each behaviour is specific to the child, the situation and how that behaviour is being handled. Each behaviour also carries its own message about the child and his or her experiences, and the best approaches are going to be those that are planned individually and based on your own observations and knowledge of the child. Two books give you a mixture of recipes and also the understanding and reflection to enable you to do your own 'cooking'.

Who the book is aimed at

This book will be helpful for early years practitioners, childminders, nursery and foundation stage teachers, managers, special educational needs co-ordinators (SENCOs) and support teachers. Parents and carers will also find the approaches very relevant and might find it useful to use the same approaches at home as those used in the nursery setting.

How to use the book

It is recommended that you read through the whole book rather than simply picking chapters of interest because one chapter builds on another. Once you are familiar with the contents, it should be possible to dip into the book for ideas of approaches. There are lists of useful books, resources and contacts at the end of the book.

Behaviour and feelings

Chapter One introduces the idea that children need to feel positively about themselves if they are to behave well. The thrust of the book is that each and every child is entitled to a full and balanced Early Years Foundation Stage (EYFS) and that it is up to early years workers to plan approaches and interventions that are going to make this possible. The book promotes an inclusive approach in which children are *not* excluded on account of their behaviour.

Ages and stages

If you are going to manage behaviour effectively, it is helpful to have a general idea about what behaviour is typical for each age and stage. This helps you to focus on changing problem behaviours rather than spotting problem children. Chapter Two covers issues surrounding expectations and how to share these. There are ideas for helping you to develop clear, unambiguous language when talking about behaviour with others.

Getting ready

Chapter Three helps you to set the scene in your setting for behaviour management. It covers the standards which you need to meet and provides background information to help you plan your behaviour policy. Behaviour management includes thinking about the whole context in which a behaviour takes place. There are, therefore, ideas for planning the environment, room management and for planning activities and routines.

Defining problems

In Chapter Four there is information to help you when a child's behaviour becomes a significant problem. Various methods of observation and assessment are described. You will already have coped with a wide range of behaviours in your setting simply because children come to you with very different experiences and levels of maturity. You will be able to manage most of these simply by patiently teaching appropriate behaviour in a positive way through the personal, social and emotional EYFS framework. However, sometimes a child's behaviour is so extreme, so immature, so disruptive or potentially dangerous that you need to plan additional or different approaches, even when that child has had time to settle in.

Planning changes

There are ideas for planning general interventions and for using behavioural approaches to bring about changes in behaviour in Chapter Five. These are based on the idea that all behaviour takes place in a context. There is, therefore, something that will have led up to and triggered the behaviour, be it in the environment or from within the child. There will also be a certain consequence of the behaviour which will affect whether that behaviour is likely to happen again. Armed with this knowledge, you can plan changes in settings or responses in order to change a difficult behaviour. There is also information on how to use rewards and praise effectively.

Supporting families

One of the most challenging aspects of working with difficult behaviour can be communicating with parents and carers in a constructive way which is going to bring everyone on board. Chapter Six covers this area and provides ideas for useful ways of talking with parents and giving them a positive job to do.

Finally, there is a list of references and resources at the back.

Chapter One

Feeling good, behaving well

Feeling successful

Children need to be confident if they are to cope with all the various challenges they will meet. Confidence and learning seem to be bound together – if a child tries something and succeeds, self-esteem and confidence are raised and they are likely to try again next time and to learn. On the other hand, if a child tries something but cannot succeed, self-esteem and confidence are lowered and they are less likely to try again next time and to learn from it. That is why it is so important that the approaches we design for helping children's behaviour and social development should remain positive and should leave the children feeling good about themselves.

Try to remember that you are dealing with difficult *behaviour* and not difficult children. Behaviour management involves reducing difficult behaviours, but also teaching children new and more appropriate ways to behave instead. Therefore, you cannot separate behaviour management from the nurturing of personal, social and emotional development.

Not all children who have behavioural, emotional or social difficulties (BESD) have boisterous and challenging behaviour – you should be just as concerned about the child who is very quiet, withdrawn or whose behaviour suddenly changes.

Children can display emotional difficulties for many different reasons. Some of these will stem from their pasts, their life changes or their relationships with others. You can read more about some of the risk factors which make children vulnerable to emotional and behavioural difficulties and how to spot children with low self-esteem in the book *Emotional Literacy and Mental Health in Early Years* (Mortimer, 2003).

Make sure that you have a basic awareness of the risk factors associated with abuse – be it physical, emotional or sexual. The need to act on any concerns about child protection override all the suggestions in this book and always need to take priority, however difficult it may be at the time.

Guiding principles

It helps if you and your colleagues share some basic principles and visions concerning your work with young children's behaviour. Here are some examples.

1) We encourage the children to behave appropriately using positive approaches which encourage their self-esteem.

2) We manage the children's behaviour with a proper respect for the children themselves and their parents or carers. We respect their culture, their ethnicity, their language, their religion, their age and their gender. The approaches we use for managing behaviour must be respectful of all children regardless of their gifts, abilities or specific learning needs.

3) Behaviour management and the personal, social and emotional education of young children are not two separate, discrete activities. As a consequence, when we work with young children's behaviour, we will attend to their whole development and lives and not to certain aspects of it.

4) We believe in the principle of the 'loving use of power'. Early years educators inevitably have power; this needs to be acknowledged and used lovingly, wisely and well.

5) The interests of the child are paramount. Changing their behaviour must enhance their lives, their learning and their development. It must 'work' for the child.

6) We also recognise that children will thrive best only if their families thrive and we aim to work in close partnership with families and the community.

Entitlements for all children

It can be a useful exercise to think about the rights and entitlements of *all* children before you start becoming too involved in what makes a particular child's behaviour difficult or different. What could a 'good' entitlement and provision look like from the children's perspective?

- Children are entitled to be cared for by a small number of familiar and consistent people who understand and are sympathetic to their needs.

- Children are entitled to opportunities to form mutually respectful relationships with a range of other children and adults.

- Children are entitled to be safe from emotional and physical harm.

- Children are entitled to a sense of well-being, to feelings of self-worth and identity and confidence in themselves as learners.

- Children are entitled to contribute their individual and unique thoughts, feelings and ideas and to be respected for the choices and decisions they make.

- Children are entitled to opportunities to take on a range of responsibilities in the setting, progressively becoming more aware of what is involved in being a member of a group.

- Children are entitled to opportunities to learn through their senses and physical activity, through active involvement in first-hand experiences and play.

- Children are entitled to express their feelings and emotional needs to others.

- Children are entitled to opportunities to think, understand, ask questions, learn skills and processes and to pursue their own interests and concerns.

- Children are entitled to opportunities to learn about themselves and others, to become critically aware, and to grow to recognise and challenge bias, stereotypes and discriminatory behaviour.

Creating the right ethos

If you accept this kind of approach based on entitlements for all children rather than a singling out of 'difficult children', then ways of creating the right ethos develop naturally. Straight away, you can see how isolating children or preventing them from playing with others are not as desirable as teaching them how to behave appropriately. It is clear from the entitlements that all children need to be supported in their learning by staff who:

- work with parents and carers with trust, respecting each other's concerns, circumstances, practices and traditions;

- are respectful of differences between individual children;

- provide an environment, indoors and outdoors, that is healthy, interesting, involving, safe and fun, and which allows children to be physical;

- have high expectations of all children's developing capabilities, giving them opportunities to take risks, to experience success and failure and to reflect on their own learning and achievements;

- value them for their religious, ethnic/racial, cultural, linguistic and sex/gender identities, and for their special needs, aptitudes and interests;

- welcome their contributions to the group and to the activities;

- sensitively extend the range of each child's responsibilities;

- listen, watch, take time to understand, welcome children's curiosity, follow where children lead, and provide time, space and opportunities for extending children's thinking, imagining and understanding;

- treat everyone with respect and equal concern.

Appropriate behaviour

What behaviour are you hoping to encourage in your early years setting? If you are going to speak of 'difficult' behaviours, it would be helpful to be clear about the appropriate behaviours you are hoping to encourage in the first place. It is probable that you would like children to be able to:

- feel motivated and confident enough to develop to their potential;

- respect themselves and other people;

- be able to make friends and gain affection;

- express their feelings in appropriate ways;

- do as they are nicely asked;

- make a useful contribution to the group;

- develop a positive self-esteem.

The EYFS framework for personal, social and emotional development describes the goals to aim for by the end of the Foundation Stage and are useful to keep in mind when developing your approaches for assessing and supporting the children's behaviour in your group.

Experience tells us that appropriate behaviour is most likely if children know what is expected of them. Some children may be coming to your setting with the idea that 'play' is synonymous with 'rough and tumble' or chasing each other around. They may need to be shown how to play appropriately, and helped to understand the right and wrong times for more physical behaviour. They usually respond best to a familiar structure with a calm and purposeful atmosphere, but it may take them a while to become familiar with your routines and to understand that sociable play can be purposeful and intrinsically rewarding.

Children also respond best where there is mutual courtesy, kindness and respect making it easier for people to work and play together. This might need to be learned in the context of your setting with the adults constantly modelling courteous and kind behaviour to each other and to the children. 'Pleases' and 'thank-yous' come much more easily when they are part of the daily exchange rather than when children are confronted with constant demands to 'say the magic word'.

Where the children are behaving appropriately towards each other, each individual enjoys maximum freedom without threatening the freedom or enjoyment of others. This will be most likely to happen when there are observant and interested adults ensuring that each child's needs are met, and where children are encouraged and supported while they learn self-discipline.

Appropriate behaviour is also more likely if positive approaches are used to raise and maintain children's self-esteem. Children who are nagged constantly with 'don't' and 'no', tend to stop listening or trying after a while, and come to see themselves as 'naughty'. Children whose appropriate behaviour is noticed and praised are more likely to repeat the behaviours which are attracting your admiration and to see themselves as helpful and kind.

Chapter Two

Sharing expectations

Ages and stages

If you have had experience of working or living with very young children, then you will know that there are wide differences in the ages at which they reach new milestones. Walking and talking are classic examples of this – without there being anything wrong with children, they might begin to walk at eight months or even almost two years. Some learn to crawl very early on and others are content to lie and watch the world go by for several months, perhaps by-passing the crawling stage altogether and perfecting an efficient 'bottom shuffle'. Some are using several single words by the time they are one. Others use very few and speak 'gobbledegook' until they are two when they suddenly produce whole phrases!

In the same way, children learn appropriate behaviour at very different stages and this will be related both to the dispositions they are born with and the experiences they meet in their world. It is constructive if you can gain a clear idea of the stages that children go through when they are learning how to behave. You will find a fuller description of the typical stages of development in the book *Personal, Social and Emotional Development of Children in the Early Years* (Mortimer, 2001) in this series.

Behaviour: what is normal?

These figures were taken from parents' descriptions of their children's behaviour and show the percentage of the age group described as having that kind of problem still. You will find more of this kind of information in *New Toddler Taming* (Green, 2006).

Behaviour			
Age	2	3	4
	%	%	%
Fights or quarrels	72	75	92
Hits others or takes things	68	52	46
Stubborn	95	92	85
Talks back cheekily	42	73	72
Disobedient	82	76	78
Tells fibs	2	26	37
Constantly seeks attention	94	48	42
Cries easily	79	53	58
Temper outbursts	83	72	70
Active – hardly ever still	100	48	40
Wets self during the day	75	14	7

From *New Toddler Taming* (Green, 2006)

Individual differences

Over the past 30 years, fashion has changed on how we view temperament and personality. At one time, personality tests were widely used and fostered a belief that you could not influence a child's behaviour much – it was all 'in the genes'. Then professionals and researchers began to see behaviour as mainly the product of the environment and pointed out that siblings brought up in very different situations developed very different patterns of behaviour. The research on early emotional attachments provided support for this idea.

Nowadays, we see both genetics and the environment as playing important roles, the one interacting with the other. Whilst children are influenced greatly by the way they live and the way in which they are brought up, we can also distinguish very different temperaments and individual differences between children even within the same families. Our genes appear to determine the ranges within which we behave – we may react to things placidly, for example, or we may become emotional very quickly, but the situation we find ourselves in determines how we will respond within that range.

Therefore, there will be times when you will meet some very determined little personalities within your setting whose behaviour can be quite a challenge to manage. There will be other children who appear almost too 'laid back' for their own good, and miss exciting opportunities for learning because of their passivity. This does not mean that children who are individually different are 'problem' children. You are probably already well practised in working with a range of different personalities and you need to bring on board all your 'people' skills in order to respond flexibly to individual differences. This is at the heart of an inclusive approach.

Seeing behaviour objectively

When you are hoping to change difficult behaviour in a child you need, first of all, to learn how to describe behaviour in clear observable terms. We can only agree that a particular behaviour has improved if we have a clear consensus about what the difficult behaviour was in the first place. Words like 'naughty' may seem clear enough to us when we use them, but will other people understand them in the same way? You can begin to see how very important different *expectations* are – one person's 'naughty' (used because a toddler is always opening cupboards to explore them) may be very different to another's (used because a four year-old is hitting out in order to get a favourite toy). This is why you will now read about how to develop clear and unambiguous language when talking about behaviour.

When you talk about children's behaviour, you should choose words which are observable and clear. In other words, the verb or action word should be seen, heard or touched. For example: 'She is being aggressive' might mean different things to different people. You could not see the moment she started and the moment she stopped, but: 'She is hitting other children' can be seen and is obvious to everyone.

One way of deciding whether a statement is clear is to apply the 'Guess what?' test. If someone can rush in from outside and say: 'Guess what?' followed by a description of what they have just seen there and if this gives you exact information about what is happening outside, then that statement was 'clear'. If you really have no idea of what they are talking about, or if you see something entirely different to them in your mind's eye, then that statement was 'cloudy'. There is a famous example often used in training which gives an example of this: 'Sally is having a meaningful relationship with the dairy executive' is cloudy. 'Sally is cuddling the milkman' is clear!

Consider these *cloudy* statements about behaviour:
- Jake's mum needs to give him much more attention.
- Gareth is always aggressive when he plays with Tariq.
- Bethany has been 'inside out' all morning.
- David thinks very carefully about what he is doing.
- Callum seems to have a persecution complex.
- Luke is hyperactive.

Compare them to these *clear* statements:
- Crystal sat still for the whole story today.
- Nicky took a toy from Carly and Carly started to cry.
- Every time Warren passes the computer he cries.
- Abdul pushed three children over today.

When you are describing children's behaviour, follow two rules:

- talk about difficult *behaviour* and not difficult children;

- use *clear* language that is unambiguous and non-judgmental.

That way, you will all agree on where you are starting from and what you hope to achieve in terms of a change in behaviour.

Chapter Three

Setting the scene

If you are going to manage behaviour effectively in your setting, you need to have a clear policy that describes your philosophy about children's behaviour, how you will set about promoting appropriate behaviour in your setting and managing inappropriate behaviour. You do not have to start from scratch – there are clear government guidelines which set out the standards all registered settings should aim to meet. The DfEE document *Full Day Care – National standards for under eights day care and childminding* (ref DfEE 0488/2001) provides you with the guidance you need for setting the ethos of your special educational needs (SEN) and behaviour policies. It also gives you criteria by which you can measure whether your setting is meeting the standards successfully. The Day Care Standards are due to form part of the Early Years Foundation Stage from 2008.

A positive behaviour policy

One of the standards states that the registered person produces a written statement on behaviour management, including bullying, which states the methods used to manage children's behaviour. This should be fully understood and followed by all staff and discussed with parents.

Each registered setting should have a behaviour policy which shows how your group promotes good behaviour using positive approaches. This should be a workable and accessible document that draws together all the things that you do in your setting that encourage good behaviour in the children. It makes common sense for it to flow out of your other policies and, in particular, the policies you have on SEN and Equal Opportunities. Usually the same factors that promote inclusion, confidence and a sense of belonging also promote good behaviour.

Here are some of those factors, though you will probably have more arising from your other policies.

- Encouraging all the children to feel enthusiastic in their learning.

- Making sure that all children and adults feel included in the setting.

- Findings ways of showing that you value each and every child.

- Supporting children as they arrive, depart and go between activities.

- Developing each child's sense of worth and confidence.

- Making sure that adults feel confident and develop skills for handling difficult behaviour.

- Making the transfer between settings or into school go smoothly.

- Finding ways in which each child can learn successfully.

- Teaching children to work and play within groups.

- Showing children how to listen to and communicate with each other.

- Building up children's concentration and teaching looking and listening skills.

- Providing positive role models, especially through the adults' own behaviour.

- Making sharing enjoyable and successful.

- Finding ways of motivating each child.

- Providing nurturing and comfort where needed.

- Working in partnership with parents and carers.

- Using approaches that have been shown to support self-esteem such as circle time.

What should your behaviour policy contain?

The policy would begin with a clear set of aims followed by details of how you would achieve those aims.

The aims of the policy

Here is a list of suggestions:

- Say that you recognise and support the principles of the various codes of practice, frameworks and standards that are currently in place.

- Comment on your learning environment. You could talk about how you provide a stimulating, calm and inclusive setting and how the staff have positive attitudes and always try to remove any barriers to learning.

- Mention how you use your resources both within the setting and beyond to help the children become active and valued members of their community.

- Mention how you ensure that staff are kept up to date with information and approaches to help them promote appropriate behaviour and manage any difficult behaviour effectively.

- Indicate how you work towards keeping the behaviour policy up to date and how you are always aiming to improve the service you provide for encouraging positive behaviour in your setting.

How to implement the policy

Your policy should then describe how you carry out the behaviour policy in your setting. Here is a list of suggestions:

- How it is ensured that all staff understand and implement the behaviour policy.

- How staff respond to children who have emotional or behaviour difficulties.

- Any particular roles and responsibilities of staff members.

- Name the person who has special responsibility and knowledge of behaviour management issues. Usually this is the SENCO, inclusion coordinator or the manager.

- List any special training in behaviour management that the staff have received and how you plan and monitor their training needs.

- State how you work with parents and carers to design, implement and review the policy.

You might find the following example helpful as a starting point.

Daisychain Nursery School

Our Behaviour Policy

Our aim
- We aim to provide a setting where each and every child feels accepted and valued.

- We want each child to feel happy and to grow in confidence, whatever their needs.

- We want all the children to develop friendly and helpful behaviour.

How we do this
- We try to make each play and learning experience enjoyable and to make sure that each child can succeed.

- We use positive praise and show the children that we value what they are doing using praise, photographs and displays.

- We warn children before an activity is going to change.

- We show them how to behave in a friendly way as well as tell them.

- We sometimes work in small groups so that we can teach the children to join in and to share.

- We use a daily circle time to teach the children personal and social skills.

- The children help us to agree just a few clear rules which we encourage the children to follow with helpful reminders.

- If we need to tell a child to behave more appropriately, we do this away from an audience whenever possible.

How we respond to children who have emotional or behaviour difficulties

- If a child does not respond to our usual approaches, we talk with the group's special educational needs co-ordinator, whose name is Ella.

- She discusses the child's behaviour with parents or carers, helps us assess what the difficulties are and helps us plan our approaches.

- We design an individual behaviour plan to suit the child, based on positive approaches.

- We can call on the advice of the Behaviour Support Teacher if needed, and always notify parents or carers first.

How we involve parents and carers

- We believe that the best approaches will come if we can use the expertise of both home and setting.

- We always value what parents and carers have to tell us about their child's behaviour and can use this information to plan our approaches.

- If a child's behaviour needs an individual approach, we will discuss and share the plan with parents and carers and review it regularly with them.

These staff have had training in behaviour management and emotional difficulties: Ella S., Zach N., Sue B.

We review this behaviour policy each September at the annual management meeting.

Planning the environment

Young children behave best when they feel secure and valued and when they are aware of the routines and boundaries in your setting. The starting point for encouraging appropriate behaviour is to think about how you structure the environment so that:

- there is a familiar structure which leads to an atmosphere of calm and a sense of purpose;

- each child will be happily engaged and at ease;

- children know what is expected of them;

- children know how to behave appropriately;

- each individual enjoys maximum freedom of choice without threatening the freedom or enjoyment of others in the group;

- there are adults who are observant and supportive, making sure that each child's needs are being met;

- there is an atmosphere of mutual courtesy, kindness and respect;

- the children are encouraged to develop self-discipline as well as to 'do as they are nicely asked';

- there are a few simple and meaningful rules that have been developed with children and families, rather than many rules with frequent confrontations;

- appropriate behaviour is noticed, valued and commended by positive staff members.

If you are going to encourage 'good' behaviour in the setting, you need to be clear about the behaviour you are hoping to encourage. It is all too easy for adults to leave well alone when children are behaving and concentrating beautifully, only to intervene when there is trouble and strife. If that is what is happening, the ultimate message to the children is that they need to misbehave in order to get attention. Adult attention is usually the strongest reinforcer they can be given when learning how to behave.

The following are the behaviours you will probably wish to encourage in your setting:

- Children and adults are kind to one another and do not hurt each other.

- Children help to look after the group's property and do not damage it.

- Children and adults respect each other and themselves.

- Children 'do as they are nicely asked'.

- Children understand and try to follow the rules, especially those on safety.

- Children learn to share and take turns with each other.

- All children join in and have access to the EYFS.

Room management

If you are going to ensure that each child's needs are being met, then you all need to be sure of your roles. It can be helpful to manage staff time effectively by each of you developing different roles. These roles can be rotated to provide everyone with the same experiences or volunteers/parent helpers might be used to provide extra pairs of hands for certain of the roles. The idea of 'room management' is important when there are several children whose behaviour is causing you concern. For example, supposing there are four adults in a room of lively two to three year-olds. You might define four distinct roles for the helpers:

- The activity facilitator, who plans and organises structured activities, engages and supports the children as they take part and stays mainly in one place for the duration of that activity.

- The play facilitator, who moves around the room supporting and engaging all the children in their choice of free play.

- The nurturer, who remains in the soft cushion area and is available for comforting and for sharing story books or songs.

- The care facilitator who moves around ensuring safety, meeting personal needs, helping the children mop up spills, managing any 'accidents', etc.

Depending on your situation, these roles may need to be combined. If a child has additional support because of their special educational needs, you might also have a support worker who has a particular eye for the needs of the child with SEN, ensuring that this child can access the EYFS and is fully included. Where the SEN involves behavioural and emotional difficulties, this role might include putting into effect any positive behaviour programme which you might have agreed for the child. Room management works best when it is used as the ideal structure and when staff are also encouraged to be flexible and use their shared expertise and common sense to support each other when necessary.

Planning activities

You will need to plan a balance of child-led play and adult-led activities. You really can avoid many behaviour problems by making sure that any activities you plan are at a suitable level for the children, suit their style of learning and that the expectations which adults have are appropriate to them. Young children, like all of us, are at different stages of maturity and developing their learning styles, and you need to plan activities which suit all of the children inclusively. For example, some older children find it easiest to attend and concentrate when they are listening. Others need to look and others still need to handle and manipulate. In the EYFS, the rule of thumb is to plan the activities in a multi-sensory way so that young children can listen and think, can observe and inspect and can also feel and manipulate. In other words, plan a learning experience which is all of these:

- visual;

- auditory;

- kinesthetic.

This also applies to how you yourselves present the learning activities. The ideal teaching style will be to:

- show the children what to do (modelling the activity or providing pictures, real objects or concrete examples);

- tell the children what to do (giving clear and simple instructions, emphasising key words or providing a simple running commentary as the child plays);

- give the children something to do (making the activity practical and encouraging the process of the learning as well as the product).

The activities themselves need to be child-centred (tuned into their values and interests), allowing the children an element of choice and helping them feel successful in their learning and playing.

Routines

Children need to feel secure within a setting and this will come from a regular and familiar routine. While you will always wish to retain the flexibility to respond to a learning opportunity as it arises ('Quick everyone! Come and look at the rainbow'), you need to aim for a familiar pattern or routine that will provide the children with the security to cope with any new changes and demands within it. This will involve a regular start and finish to your session. It will also involve regular and stable staff members with whom the children can feel familiar.

It is good practice in all settings for teachers or managers to adopt a 'key person' system. A named adult has particular care and concern for a small group of children. This might allow you to have smaller group times within the larger group session and provide a 'secure base' from which the children can operate and play. Within the smaller group, staff can provide nurturing, can help the children plan and review their day, can use a regular welcome and farewell circle time, and can keep a watchful eye to make sure that each child is fully included. Children can be encouraged to make choices in their play and conflicts can be handled with guidance and support.

Staying safe

Your particular knowledge of a child's behaviour is bound to influence how you plan for everyone's safety. Under the SEN Disability Act, you will be expected to make 'reasonable adjustments' for any child who has a significant difficulty on account of behavioural or emotional needs. On a day-to-day basis, there are many considerations that will help keep you 'a step ahead' of incidents that might affect safety:

- Make sure your premises are secure to keep unwanted visitors out and energetic children in.

- Make sure that physical play is supervised and safety matting is used where appropriate with large equipment.

- If a child throws objects continuously, remove dangerous items and supervise the safety of younger children.

- If major tantrums are a problem, try to set up a quiet area for a member of staff and the child to withdraw to for 'cooling off'.

- If there is a lot of kicking, consider encouraging slippers for the children.

- Make sure you are all trained in lifting and handling techniques.

- Use safety gates on kitchen spaces or stairways and safety catches on closed cupboards.

- You will all need to have the appropriate police and health checks.

- You need to be kept regularly up-to-date with child protection procedures.

- Use risk management approaches to provide additional supervision and support for children whose behaviour is a risk to themselves or to others.

Chapter Four

Problem behaviour

You will already have developed your own practices for handling the children's behaviour in your group or setting and these should be along the lines of your behaviour policy. They will work for most children most of the time. However, there will be times when you feel that your usual approaches are not working and that an inappropriate behaviour has become somewhat 'stuck'. This chapter deals with the issues of *how* you decide when a behaviour becomes a problem and *what* to do next.

If you have a child in your setting whose behaviour is causing concern, ask yourselves these questions before you decide on whether there really is a problem:

- *Has the child had time to settle into your group or setting?* Some children take longer than others to settle into new routines, so the behaviour might settle once the child is used to your setting.

- *Has anyone talked with parents or carers yet?* They know their child 'inside out' and can contribute useful information and ideas. What they say might allay your fears or at least help you to understand what is going on. Perhaps there are changes at home that will inevitably leave the child unsettled for a while. What they say might also lead you to feel that you need to use more special approaches or advice. You always need to be vigilant for any child protection issues and follow your usual procedures.

- *Have you considered that poor self-esteem and confidence might be at the root of things?* If so, use a key worker to befriend and support the child, using positive encouragement and support to enable them to feel more confident and 'tuned in' to you all.

- *Has the child not yet learned to play calmly and socially?* This might not be a behaviour 'problem', but more a case of teaching the child another way to play and behave. Look for strategies to make play extra fun, and rules clear. Play alongside the child with one or two other children showing that playing socially can be 'safe' and enjoyable.

- *Is the child not yet at a developmental stage where he or she has learned sharing, turn-taking and asking for things etc?* It might be that the behaviour 'problem' is related to the fact that the child is still at a young stage of development.

You can find out more about the 'problem' by trouble-shooting and finding out which approaches help you begin to see an improvement. Identifying a behaviour problem and planning an intervention should be inextricably bound together so that knowledge of the one informs the other. You will find ideas for planning a range of interventions in Chapter 5. Start by choosing a few clear rules which the children have contributed to. Talk about them during circle time. Look for opportunities to praise children specifically ('Thank you for giving that crayon to Freddy') for following the rules. Help children who do not, by showing them what to do instead and then praising them.

If a child has had time to settle with you and still is not responding to your usual encouragement and boundary setting, despite all the approaches above, then you might consider talking to parents about using approaches which are additional or different to the usual. Consider planning 'Early Years Action' and putting together a within-setting individual behaviour plan (see page 49).

Criteria for problem behaviour

There are four main criteria for helping you to decide whether a behaviour is problematical:

1) *Fixation*: a behaviour has continued beyond the age where it might be considered appropriate. For example, many one year-olds throw toys, but it becomes a problem if a four year-old regularly throws them.

2) *Regression*: a behaviour might have been achieved successfully at an appropriate age and the child then reverts back to behaviour characteristic of a younger age. For example, a child might have settled beautifully into the setting and then begins to cry inconsolably for no apparent reason.

3) *Failure to display*: a behaviour which should have developed by a particular age has not done so. For example, a four year-old might find it impossible to share or to take turns without lashing out, or to separate from a main carer without screaming.

4) *Exaggeration*: a normal behaviour such as a burst of temper might become exaggerated into a full-blown temper tantrum in which other children get hurt. Also, a behaviour might become greatly exaggerated in order to gain attention, such as hitting younger children.

Talking with parents or carers

It is one thing to share expectations of the children's behaviour and progress with your colleagues, it is another to work in partnership with parents and carers to establish a common language and expectation about their children's behaviour. How can you share your own expectations between home and setting? Look for opportunities to share with parents and carers what activities you are doing in the session and why – this all helps to give them clearer expectations about what stage their child has reached. For example: 'Young children have to be taught how to share so we play simple turn-taking games to make this fun'; 'Most children use silly words if they notice people paying them attention. That is why you will find us ignoring some words they say'. Other suggestions include:

- Share the behaviour problem chart on page 15. This can be a real eye-opener to parents who might feel that their child is the only one with the problem.

- Use positive questioning to find out the parents' or carers' views on the problem: 'How do you feel he is doing in the group?'; 'What's going well?'; What's his favourite thing here?'; 'When does he behave best?'; 'What helps him do that?'; 'What do you think would make a difference to his behaviour in the group?'.

- Be aware of any cultural or religious reasons why parents and carers might view a behaviour problem differently from you. For example, parents might feel that it is right for their child to hit another child back or wrong for their child to join in with a physical game. Respect the framework they are using and explain clearly what you need to achieve in the setting, seeking a mutually agreed compromise if necessary. Seek advice from your local multi-cultural education service if appropriate.

- Encourage visits to the group by parents and carers so that they can see how you manage a behaviour and use it to explain why, without suggesting that parents are 'bad parents' if they are not doing the same thing.

- Explain that children can learn to behave very differently in different situations.

- Ask if there are concerns that they have about their child's behaviour which you might work on together.

- If a parent or carer sees a problem behaviour as a problem child and is very negative about them, patiently rephrase the statements in terms of what the child is doing (rather than what they are). You can also plan interventions which improve family relationships and work on how parents view and relate to their child. Setting play tasks to share together at home usually works well.

- Plan events where you can talk about a particular aspect of your play and behaviour policy together so that you are all informed with the same knowledge of ages and stages.

- If there is an entrenched problem with a child's behaviour, make sure that you involve parents and carers from the early stages and involve them in your planning and consultation.

- If there are entrenched problems in communicating with parents and carers, keep a record of what you have tried and seek general advice from outside professionals in an attempt to look for creative and innovative ways to overcome them.

- Make links with any local Sure Start scheme so that you can work together on the expectations that local families and carers have of their young children.

- Above all, share the pleasures of the caring as well as the problems. Show that you like and respect their child and build on the fact that you both wish the best for that child.

Observation and assessment

The first step with a behaviour difficulty is to gather information through talking with the family, any other professional involved and through observing the behaviour itself. Not only does this provide you with useful information but it gives you 'thinking time' to work out what you can do about it. Once a problem has been identified everyone will be looking towards you to 'do something'. When you gather information, you are clearly doing something even though you do not have a plan of action formulated. Sometimes the very act of standing back a little and observing what is going on gives you the emotional distance needed to think about the problem more objectively. There are various ways in which you can observe and record problem behaviour. When this is done prior to a behavioural intervention, it is called collecting 'baseline' information.

S.T.A.R. chart

Keep a diary recording what the child was actually doing, what seemed to lead up to it and what the consequences were. Write clearly and objectively, describing observable actions and using non-judgmental language (see page 16). This is called a S.T.A.R. chart because it records the:

- *Setting* (what happened before the behaviour took place, the context, the situation at the time);

- *Trigger* (what seemed to set the behaviour off);

- *Action* (exactly what the child did);

- *Response* (what happened as a result of the behaviour or what those around the child did next).

It is helpful if you can have 'good news' and 'bad news' diary sheets so that you can gather information about activities and sessions that went really successfully as well as those that went badly. In this way you come to see what interventions actually work already.

Counting or measuring the behaviour

Sometimes a behaviour is so evident that you can actually count the number of times it happens during a session. This is only possible if you have all agreed together what constitutes the problem behaviour and when you will count it as happening. One staff member's 'temper tantrum' could be another's 'grumble' – in other words two people can observe the same child doing the same behaviour and describe or interpret it in very different ways. Behaviours which might lend themselves to a frequency count include, for example, throwing toys, upsetting toy boxes, kicking, and climbing onto the tables.

Other behaviours can be measured in terms of their duration – perhaps a child screamed for 10 minutes today or played happily for 20 minutes continuously. The whole point of measuring the behaviour in some way is to enable you to:

- see change;

- monitor the intervention you have planned.

Unless you have recorded that you started with six major temper tantrums each session and that you are now (three weeks later) down to three, you would never appreciate the success you are having. Instead, you would have become so focused on these temper tantrums that you would be wondering why, after all your hard work, they were still very much in evidence. Only by seeing that you have in fact reduced them by half can you assume that you are probably working on the right lines.

Spot observations

With older children we sometimes use spot observations to see whether a child is 'off task' or 'on task'. This becomes meaningless in the early years setting because all play is 'on task' and learning and play should be synonymous. However, there are occasions when this can be a very helpful approach, depending on the behaviour being observed. For example, you could collect spot observations. Supposing that you were worried about a child whose behaviour was very solitary. Every five minutes you could observe the child briefly and record whether he was playing on his own or with others. This would give you a baseline against which you could measure positive change. Perhaps your baseline observations show that the child was playing on his own for 10/12 observations. After you have worked on encouraging more group and social play, you might be able to record a 'post baseline' of only 3/12. The whole observation need only take one hour of quick five minute spot checks. Repeat it in different situations and in different sessions so that you are sure you have a meaningful sample.

'Fly on the wall' observation

If you have the opportunity, observe a child over a continuous period of time (say 30 minutes) and write down what they are doing and how they are interacting in clear, unambiguous terms. Record the time in the left hand margin so that you will have an idea of how long the child was playing in a specific area, with certain children, or demonstrating a particular behaviour.

Where possible, arrange for extra help so that you can be released for this length of time. Ask other staff members to carry on as if you were not present and not to rely on you to manage any incidents or help the children. Sit somewhere to the side of the room and move discretely from area to area in order to keep the child in view.

It soon becomes possible to develop the knack of observing from the corner of one's eye and recording as you watch. If other children approach, keep your eyes down and explain briefly but politely: 'I'm doing my writing today. You will need to ask . . . instead'. Later, you can look through the observation together with other staff members and identify any patterns to the behaviour.

If you are a childminder, try to keep running notes as you both play with and observe the child at play – this is called a 'participant observation'.

Chapter Five

Planning interventions

When a child's behaviour is particularly problematical, it is likely that those of you who are trying to deal with this are already feeling stressed, emotionally vulnerable and perhaps defensive. You may feel that you are being asked for 'the answer' and you, too, may be left feeling frustrated and inadequate. All of these feelings can lead towards exclusion rather than inclusion of the child and the child's individual needs. It can be helpful to bear these points in mind:

- There are no 'right answers' – only individual solutions. Therefore, it helps to explore each situation and come up with the best ways forward.

- You will become a more effective manager of behaviour if you reflect on the problem behaviour and work out some of the solutions yourself. Try not to rely exclusively on 'recipe book' approaches.

Behaviour management

Behaviour management is just one of the many tools that you can use in order to change difficult behaviour. You would feel uncomfortable basing your entire EYFS teaching around the premise that children only behave in a certain way in order to gain rewards. However, there is a definite place for it when a particular child is displaying very difficult and demanding behaviour which has not responded to your usual approaches. In other words, you have already decided that something 'additional and different' is required. It gives you a definite job to do at a time when you might be feeling disempowered or lacking in confidence because of a child's behaviour.

Behaviour management is based on the theory of behavioural psychology and makes use of positive encouragement and reward. In essence, a 'behavioural' theory states that:

- If you do something, and something *pleasant* happens to you, you are more likely to do that thing again.

- If you do something, and something *unpleasant* happens to you, you are less likely to do that thing again.

So far, this should make sense to everyone. Suppose, for example, that you move to a new job and pluck up courage on the first day to say hello to a new colleague in the corridor. If that person smiles and says hello back, then you are likely to continue with a regular greeting and perhaps get to know each other better over time. However, if the person looks away and does not reply, then you are likely to feel less confident and not so likely to greet the person the next time you meet. In other words, what happens to you affects what you are likely to do in the future.

What of the child whose behaviour becomes worse after a 'good telling off'? Should it not follow that when something unpleasant happens (like the telling off) the child is likely to behave *better*? In reality, we all know that this does not always follow! For some children, behaviour is an attempt to attract *any* kind of reaction or attention, even if it comes in the form of a strong reprimand. In other words, you cannot decide that the telling off is a punishment for the child unless it actually reduces the behaviour. Each child and each situation will be different.

It is helpful, therefore, to understand that rewards are not rewards because of what they *are* (eye contact and a cuddle, a clap in front of all the other children, a special food treat), but because of what they *do* (they make the behaviour *more* likely to happen in the future). Similarly, negative consequences are not simply negative because of what they *are* (a reprimand, a telling off, being sent to another room), but because of what they *do* (make the behaviour *less* likely to happen in the future).

- The pleasant event is called a *reward*, simply because it makes the behaviour *increase*.

- The unpleasant event is called a *negative consequence* simply because it makes the behaviour *decrease*. Nowadays we use the expressions 'negative consequences' or 'sanctions' instead of 'punishments' because there are less overtones of physical violence or negative action.

- Negative consequences need not be something unpleasant that happens; they can simply be that the child was expecting a certain reward to happen and it never did (for example, the temper tantrum did not bring the expected tractor ride, or the bite did not lead to being able to play with the train).

Staying positive

It sometimes comes as a surprise that we should be using *positive* approaches to dealing with what might appear to be very *negative* behaviours. Positive behavioural approaches do the following:

- They make sure that the child's self-esteem remains positive. This is because the child is given the message that it is the *behaviour* which is unacceptable, rather than the child.

- They are based on the use or removal of rewards and pleasant things. Negative consequences may work in the short-term to control or stop a difficult behaviour, but they will not help the child to change behaviour in the longer term. Instead, they lead to children behaving inappropriately until an adult intervenes, rather than learning self-control.

- They aim not only to remove or alter an inappropriate behaviour, but to replace it with a more positive and appropriate behaviour. Since you are all in the business of delivering the EYFS framework for personal, social and emotional development this makes obvious sense. You know that children do not arrive in your setting with good behaviour ready packaged – behaviour and social skills need to be learned and developed just like everything else.

Using rewards effectively

When you think about it, rewards are happening all the time in your setting. Adults smile at children, give them eye contact, make approving comments and give encouragement. All these are done quite naturally and provide motivation for the child to behave in that way again. Day by day, children receive the message that kindness, creativity, happy and constructive play, and friendly conversation are all behaviours which are regularly rewarded and valued by the people around them. There are several different categories of rewards which the children will already be used to in their daily lives.

- Social praise – smiles, eye contact, a cuddle, praise, laughter, clapping hands, cheering.

- Food and drink – favourite snacks, drinks, fruit, meals.

- Toys and playthings – being able to play with the digger, the group's Teddy, enjoying a new set of toys.

- Activities – going to play outside, having the slide out, enjoying a story, playing on the computer.

- Sights and sounds – a musical CD, a kaleidoscope, coloured lights.

- Physical – a cuddle, a swing, a brush of the hair, a gentle blowing of a fan.

If you see that rewards are a fact of daily life then you will feel more comfortable about using rewards in order to change particularly challenging behaviour. If a reward is going to be *effective* it has to satisfy these conditions:

- It must happen immediately. It is no good saying: 'You can have a treat next week'. Young children need your praise and recognition straight away.

- It must be something which catches the child's attention. It is no good saying: 'That's wonderful Ruben' in a quiet deadpan voice that Ruben will not even notice. Sometimes (with some children for whom praise has not been given regularly) you have to be extreme in your expression: 'That's FANTASTIC Ruben!'

- It has to work for the child. Some children (perhaps because they have social or autistic spectrum difficulties) genuinely find eye contact and strong praise difficult to handle. It might even cause them to behave in a way to avoid it. In other words, one child's reward might be another child's sanction.

- It has to be given consistently at first. When you are introducing behavioural approaches, you need to realise that you should reward or praise every single time a child behaves in the targeted way at first. Later, as the new behaviour becomes established, rewards can be given every now and again and gradually phased out.

- If a concrete reward (such as food or a toy) is given, perhaps because that is the only thing a child will work for at first, then social praise should always be given as well. In time, the concrete reward can be faded out as the social praise remains. In time, the child will come to find the social praise alone to be rewarding. When they are older, the aim is for them to be behaving in the appropriate way through self-control and self-discipline.

- You can use your own knowledge and experience of the child in order to work out which rewards will be effective. Parents and carers will also be a useful source of information. Perhaps their child collects certain stickers at home or loves a certain play activity. Perhaps they are on their very best behaviour when they are looking after their pet. Perhaps they love yoghurt snacks. Perhaps they love to be the family clown and be cheered and applauded. Remember that each child is unique and different.

Planning changes

The best way to change children's behaviour is to change what you, as an adult, are doing. Here are some simple steps to help you design a simple behaviour management programme in order to change a particularly difficult behaviour.

Step 1: Describe the behaviour(s) you are concerned about
Use clear language to reach agreement with colleagues and parents so that you are all clear about the behaviour you wish to work on.

Step 2: Observe the behaviour
If you are going to change a difficult behaviour into a more appropriate one, you need to know where you started from and when you have 'got there'. Your starting point is called the 'baseline'. It gives you a clear picture of how difficult or frequent the behaviour was before you started your plan to change things. You can measure behaviour in the different ways suggested on page 33. You should end up with a clearer picture of the settings, the triggers, the actions and the responses.

Step 3: Gather information
It is helpful to find out more about the child's behaviour in different situations. Speaking with parents or carers is the obvious starting point. Behaviour can sometimes be a sensitive area to discuss with families without arousing defensive feelings (there are more ideas about this in Chapter 6). There might also be useful information to be gleaned from any other professionals involved such as a health visitor, family support worker, community worker, social worker or child psychologist. Perhaps the child used to attend another group; what was the behaviour like then and what approaches helped?

Step 4: Select just one behaviour to work on first
When you gather information about a child's behaviour, you might end up with a whole list of difficult behaviours and situations. This can appear daunting unless you understand that the best place to start is on just *one* behaviour – perhaps one that is easy to change (such as running into the kitchen area) or one that is causing most disruption (such as

biting). You can reassure them that this approach can help other behaviours too by starting a 'positive spiral' of better behaviour, more positive self-esteem and a happier child.

Step 5: Decide on a hypothesis

What do you all think is keeping that behaviour going? Is the child behaving like this to seek attention? Is it because the child cannot yet play co-operatively? Is it because the child has not yet learned to share? Is it when Mum brings the child to the group and not Gran?

Step 6: Draw up a plan to change the setting, the trigger, the action or the responses

There are more ideas below and also a range of more specific interventions in the book *An A-Z of Tricky Behaviours in the Early Years* (Mortimer, 2006) in this series.

Step 7: Monitor progress over three weeks and then review your hypothesis and your interventions if you need to

Behavioural approaches take a little time to work. If, for example, you have drawn up a plan to reduce attention-seeking behaviour by reducing the amount of eye contact and reaction you are giving the child, the behaviour is likely to become worse before it becomes better since the child will be testing the boundaries for a while.

Changing the setting and trigger

What are the most common approaches you can follow for changing the setting (or context) of a difficult behaviour?

Avoid likely situations

You may have begun to see a pattern emerging. Perhaps the child behaves worst in particular situations or places, or with particular children or staff members. Perhaps the child becomes disruptive during story time, or very silly in front of certain helpers. You can break the cycle of the difficult behaviour by avoiding the situation altogether for a while. There is an element of any difficult behaviour which becomes a habit, and it is helpful to set up the situation differently so that the habit is broken for a while. It also helps everyone, child and staff alike, to feel more relaxed and confident about things. You are not being defeated in this; this is clever management because you should then have a plan to move the child towards the stage when they can cope without misbehaving. For example, if a child cannot tolerate close proximity from certain children without fighting them, you can distract them away from those children for a while, but later set up structured and supported play activities where you are helping them learn other ways of playing together.

Distract rather than confront

Distraction is one of the most powerful tools we have for managing young children's behaviour. Just at the moment when a squabble is brewing, we direct their attention to a new exciting event or opportunity, defusing the situation altogether. Once again, do not feel you are side-stepping the issue – it is clever management to use distraction in early years settings. Remember to note 'problem times' and plan other opportunities for helping the children learn more appropriate ways of behaving.

Make sure the activity suits the child's level

So often, children who are referred to support services with behaviour difficulties turn out to be experiencing difficulties in learning as well. It is also true that many children are seen to have behaviour problems simply because the expectations on them are too high. A classic example is the tall, rather active and boisterous two year-old who is perceived by adults to be older than he is. If you respond to his behaviour as you would a four year-old, that child is going to find it hard to 'get things right'. Another example would be a child who has not yet learned how to concentrate for longer than a minute or two who is expected to sit at a table and complete a worksheet.

Get full attention before giving directions

If necessary, bend down to the child's level, say their name, or gently touch their chin to ensure eye contact before giving instructions. Young children find it hard to realise that instructions given to a whole group also mean them, so you need to cue individual children in first to what you are about to say. Very active children tend to act without thinking and you will need to teach *looking* and *listening* skills before you can expect the children to pay attention to what you are saying.

Give more positive attention before the trouble starts

Many children who appear to seek a lot of attention genuinely need a great deal of positive attention. Look for ways of providing that attention when these children are behaving appropriately (they do not have to be especially good) and target your praise specifically: 'Thank you for sharing the dough, Sam'. You may find that certain children behave more appropriately for some staff than others, and it could be that some staff members tend to give more attention to misdemeanors than to appropriate behaviour.

Give a warning of changes of activity

Young children get so engrossed in what they are doing and have not learned to attend to more than one thing at a time. It can be very helpful if you give regular warnings about what is about to happen so that the children have a chance to prepare themselves for a change of activity: 'Nearly time to tidy up now – then you can play outside'.

Anticipate problem times and be a step ahead

Difficult behaviours often occur when children are in a 'vacuum' between activities, or waiting for something to happen such as at 'going home' time. Make sure the children know not only what they can be doing *now*, but what they can do *next*. Helping children to plan and review their activities is a useful strategy here. You can also use visual timetables (a sequence of photographs illustrating the key activities and routines of the session) as a way of focusing certain children on what comes next. If a child with poor listening skills finds group story time difficult, then plan ahead by asking a helper to take him/her into the book corner for an individual story time. Then gradually increase the number of children there until that child can listen within a group.

Give clear directions

Children need full reasons and explanations if they are to learn about their worlds, yet there may be times when that is not appropriate. Choose what you want to say, for example: 'No kicking' and repeat that over, making the rule simple and clear. This is sometimes known as the 'broken record approach'! Sometimes, the more that you elaborate, the more attention you are giving the child for behaving inappropriately. Instead, look for other times of day when you can talk together about reasons for behaving in a certain way and about behaving kindly.

Show the child what to do as well as saying it
Young children are usually too absorbed in what they are doing to respond to adult directions from across the room. If you are working with young children whose attention is short, approach these children and model to them what to do. These children might also find adult language difficult to understand, so add meaning to your words by showing children what to do as well. For example, if a child throws the toys into the box at tidy-up time, show the child how to make a game of 'parking' the cars gently, or putting the musical instruments back so that not a sound is made.

Choose a few simple rules and stick to them
These are especially useful when the children have contributed to them too, perhaps as a circle time activity. Stick to three or four rules at the most, perhaps relating to not hurting others, to being kind and to listening. Spend time with the children talking together about what it means to be kind and to help.

Changing the action
You can also plan interventions that directly affect the child's behaviour.

Stop it if you can
Some behaviours can be anticipated and stopped from happening. If you know ahead of time that a lively child is going to join your setting who tends to behave impulsively and has little sense of danger, then you would make sure that your boundaries, doors and gates were totally secure. You might need to fit safety locks to certain cupboards and you would carry out a risk assessment of how safe your setting was, making sure that safety features such as electric plug covers were all in place.

You can also take a look at the way your spaces are organised. Wide open spaces with wheeled toys call out to lively children to move at great speed.

Look for ways of dividing large spaces into smaller ones so that the children can enjoy quiet, focused play as well as physical activity.

Teach the child a new behaviour opposite to the first

When a child is playing constructively with another child on the car mat, s/he cannot be fighting at the same time. In other words, some behaviours are incompatible with others. You can use this fact to great advantage. Decide ahead what behaviours you wish to see in place of the problem behaviour and then set this as a target for teaching. Now you have a *positive* plan of action and are not focusing entirely on the negative behaviour. For example, you might decide to work hard to build up a child's level of concentration, to help him or her play in a supervised group or help him/her play alongside another child. In other words, you are managing the difficult behaviour by delivering social skills training or using positive teaching.

Praise another behaviour incompatible with the first

Sometimes a child is demonstrating appropriate and friendly behaviour as well as the difficult behaviour. This gives you a clear starting point for behaviour management. Use all the approaches already discussed to plan situations that make the problem behaviour less likely to happen, and then selectively praise and give attention at times when the child is behaving appropriately. There will still be good times and bad times, but usually the proportion of good times steadily increases.

Changing the responses

The third option is to plan interventions which change the consequences of a child's behaviour making it less likely to occur in the future.

Be absolutely consistent

This is the most difficult part of behaviour management. If it is to work effectively, you need to be consistent in your approaches. You can feel confused by a child's difficult behaviour and it is tempting to try one approach and then switch to another when it does not work immediately. You need to draw up a plan and to stick to it for at least three weeks. If a child hits, kicks or bites, then the same response must happen every single time, whoever the person supervising and whatever the situation, otherwise the children will learn that they can behave in a certain way if they make enough fuss or if they choose their audience or the situation.

Reward when the child is not doing the inappropriate behaviour

As well as focusing on the behaviour to be changed, you will need to think of a list of behaviours which the child would be showing when behaving appropriately instead. These behaviours should be both noticed and rewarded by you. For example, if you are planning an approach to stop Kieran from biting, then you might note that whenever Kieran was sitting at a table activity, or whenever he was sharing the water play he did not bite. You should then give attention and praise Kieran for playing well at these times. When praising the behaviour, you should focus on the positive behaviour: 'Well done for sharing', and *not* on the negative: 'Well done for not biting'.

Ignore attention-seeking behaviour where safe to do so

If a child is constantly using 'swearing' as a means of gaining a reaction from you all, this can be embarrassing and difficult to manage. Experience tells us that swearing responds best to an ignoring approach, yet you might feel you must be seen to respond and correct it. Instead, try to make it fun to behave appropriately and encourage other children to ignore silliness. So often, children who show difficult behaviour have become used to gaining attention and reaction for behaving inappropriately rather than appropriately. Try to understand that you are in the business of changing the balance of attention so that it becomes more attention-getting and fun for the child to behave appropriately than to misbehave.

Star charts and stickers can also work well

These are usually most effective when a child is about four, but they can also be used with younger children if they help. They serve the purpose of letting the child know that they are behaving appropriately at a particular moment in time and serve as a concrete recognition of their efforts. As such, they should not be removed for subsequent bad behaviour that might occur very soon after receiving the sticker. Stickers should not be overused and can be faded out gradually as new patterns of behaviour become established.

Children with special educational needs

Sometimes a child's behaviour becomes so difficult to manage that you run out of your usual approaches and interventions. This is the point for those of you in registered settings to consider discussing SEN approaches with the parents and carers. You would need to draw up an individual behaviour plan as part of your Early Years Action or Early Years Action Plus. You can read more about these SEN approaches in *The SEN Code of Practice in Early Years Settings* (Mortimer, 2002) also in this series. You can also find out more from your local Sure Start or local education authority who can support you with more specialist assessment and advice.

There are also some children whose SEN have already been identified who have certain recognised conditions that affect their behaviour. There are other books in this series that you will find helpful such as *Autistic Spectrum Disorders in the Early Years* (Jordan, 2002) and *Supporting Children with AD/HD and Attention Difficulties in the Early Years* (Mortimer, 2002). All that you have read about behaviour management will still be absolutely relevant, but a deeper understanding of the conditions will help you see where the behaviour might be coming from and what interventions are likely to be most effective.

Chapter Six

Supporting parents and carers

Talking with parents

It is not easy talking with a parent or carer about their child's behaviour. There are all sorts of emotions and defensiveness that can be aroused and it helps if you can 'tune in' to some of the emotional reactions likely to be experienced by parents.

Guilt

Parents might be wondering what they did wrong, or feeling that you are blaming them in some way for the fact that their child has a behaviour problem.

It helps to emphasise how much you value parents' help and advice in helping you manage the difficult behaviour: 'Thank you so much for coming to talk. We are having some difficulties in managing Tara's temper tantrums. It's clear that she gets quite upset with us all and we are keen to make her sessions happier for her. You know her better than anyone, so it will be really useful to talk'.

Blame

Parents may find it easiest to blame other people for the problem, perhaps even suggesting that their child learned to swear or become aggressive from the setting. They may report that there are no such problems at home and so the problem must lie in the way staff are managing the situation.

It might help to comment: 'That's interesting that there are no problems like this at home. I wonder if she only behaves like this when she has to do something she doesn't want to or when there are lots of other children around – like when she is expected to share the toys here?'

Parents and carers may also have rigid ideas about discipline and blame you for not having the same ideas ('All he needs is a good smack!'). It helps to explain clearly what you are and are not allowed to do and explain why: 'The law does not allow us to smack your child. This is because we now know that smacking encourages children to hurt others and we have to treat children with the same respect as we would anyone else. It is also our policy to use positive approaches which will help your child's emotional development in the long term'.

Protectiveness

Parents may feel very protective towards their child and jump to their child's defence. They may also feel that they have made a mistake in sending their child to you and that you might not be able to cope with their child as they have. They may also find it hard to share the responsibility of their child's behaviour with you in the setting and therefore to lose control of what is happening.

A 'no blame' problem-solving approach works best in which you make it clear that it is the *behaviour* which is the problem and *not* the child: 'We would like to work with you to change Kerry's behaviour. What do you think will work best?'

Anger

Individuals whose self-esteem is low, who feel threatened in some way or who have had negative experiences of professional 'power' may become quickly angry. Look after your own safety (if you belong to a professional association then this should have guidelines for you). It also helps to have established a working relationship with parents long before you are in the position of having to share any 'bad news'. In this way, you cease to become a threat because you are someone who is already accepted and trusted.

Grief

Sometimes you might raise a fairly minor behaviour problem with a parent or carer only to be taken by surprise by an outpouring of grief. You can never know where someone's emotions might be coming from and there may be good reasons why this is happening. Other parents may avoid even meeting you or talking about the problem because they are not sure how they will cope. It helps to allow plenty of time to work through any emotion and address all concerns in a practical and helpful way.

Anxiety

Some parents and carers may appear over anxious about their child. They may have their own difficulties in separating from their child and find it hard to trust you.

Rejection of the problem

Parents and carers may feel that they do not want to be the sort of people who have this sort of child and so they act as if it is not happening. Sometimes this gets bound in with the rejection of any kind of label and an expressed wish that their child should not be treated any differently from the other children. It helps if you can make it clear that you are not keen to label the child either, but that you *are* very keen to help the child behave more appropriately and become a happy, socially adjusted individual.

Helplessness and denial

Sometimes when family members are stressed or depressed, you may find avoidance or denial from parents and carers: 'I'm rushing off and can't talk'; 'It will all be all right'; 'He's just like Uncle Dennis was'; 'It's just the way she is'. Other parents and carers may be out of tune with their child's difficulties, perhaps because child and parent are 'unconnected' or have attachment difficulties. In this situation, it can appear to you as if they simply do not care.

Useful approaches

- Try to understand why a parent or carer might be saying something. What does this tell you about their emotional state and how you might help?

- If there is avoidance of the issue, try to take time to share the good news of progress before you need to share the challenges. Give clear information about your expectations in order to inform a parent about what you hope to achieve at each age and stage. This will lead on to what you are going to plan together for those areas that are showing a weakness.

- Involve parents and carers in the sessions wherever possible so they can see what you are trying to achieve. Try not to share only the activities, but share also the reasoning behind them and an idea of how children typically progress. Try to share some of your enthusiasm in the way children play and learn and to pass on skills.

- For helpless or troubled parents try to give practical, workable advice, but try and ensure that you do not give the impression that you are the successful ones and parents are failing – parents with low self-esteem are quick to pick up the fact that they are 'not doing it right'. This leads to resentfulness and avoidance. Instead, negotiate any home-setting activities and be encouraging and warm: 'What seems to keep his attention at home?'; 'What do you find works best when she behaves like this?'; 'When do you find he behaves best?'; 'What help do you need from us?'

- If a parent or carer denies there is anything wrong, start with where they are 'at' in terms of their understanding, but make it clear what might happen next: 'I'm glad you're not worried about her. But we must teach her to sit and listen in the group, even if she's fine at home, because she needs to be able to do this by the time she starts school. So perhaps we can talk about what seems to work at home and we'll put together a plan to teach her to concentrate here. As you say, she may settle very quickly. If not, we'll talk again next term and plan what to do next'. Be firm, stick to your plan, and continue to involve parents and carers with every sign of progress or need, making it clear that you are doing this in order to keep them in touch.

- If a parent will not stop to talk, negotiate a home visit to meet on their territory. Start with establishing their views and feelings; this gives you important information about their value judgements which will help you decide how to introduce your own concerns. Listen first, talk later, and find the common ground last. The common ground is usually your mutual like of their child that is 'special' to both of you.

53

- If parents appear over anxious, try to take their views seriously and, point by point, reassure with concrete evidence that all is well.

- Wherever possible, give parents a 'job to do'; suggestions for home are an excellent starting point.

- What if other parents are discriminating? 'If that child continues to attend, I'll take mine away'. This is a direct challenge to your special needs, behaviour and equal opportunities policies. This goes against the spirit of the SEN Disability Act and cannot be 'fudged' even though you might well understand the parent's fears or state of misinformation. Explain that it is your policy to welcome all children regardless of special need. State clearly what steps you are taking (in general terms rather than personal details) to make sure the other children's needs are not compromised (e.g. in the case of a child with severe behaviour problems).

- Consider arranging a session for everyone on 'managing difficult behaviour' or 'rising to the challenge' – usually every parent, carer (and professional!) have their challenging moments at some stage and this can be a very levelling and unifying experience for everyone.

References

DfES (2001) *Full Day Care: National standards for under eights day care and childminding* (soon to be incorporated into the Early Years Foundation Stage guidance). Nottingham: DfES Publications (ref DfEE 0488/2001).

DfES (2001) *The Special Educational Needs Code of Practice*. Nottingham: DfES Publications (ref DfES 581/2001).

DfES (2001) *Promoting Children's Mental Health within Early Years and School Settings*. Nottingham: DfES Publications (DfES ref. 0112/2001.

Jordan, R. (2002) *Autistic Spectrum Disorders in the Early Years*. Stafford: QEd Publications.

Mortimer, H. (2001) *The Observation and Assessment of Children in the Early Years*. Stafford: QEd Publications.

Mortimer, H. (2001) *Personal, Social and Emotional Development of Children in the Early Years*. Stafford: QEd Publications.

Mortimer, H. (2002) *The SEN Code of Practice in Early Years Settings*. Stafford: QEd Publications.

Mortimer, H. (2002) *Supporting Children with AD/HD and Attention Difficulties in the Early Years*. Stafford: QEd Publications.

Mortimer, H. (2003) *Emotional Literacy and Mental Health in the Early Years*. Stafford: QEd Publications.

Mortimer, H. (2006) *An A-Z of Tricky Behaviours in the Early Years*. Stafford: QEd Publications.

Useful books

Collins, M. (2001) *Circle Time for the Very Young*. Bristol: Lucky Duck Publishing.

Green, C. (1997) *New Toddler Taming: A Parent's Guide to the First Four Years*. London: Vermilion.

Merrett, F. (1997) *Positive Parenting*. Stafford: QEd Publications.

Mortimer, H. (1998) *Learning through Play: Circle Time*. Leamington Spa: Scholastic.

Quinn, M. and T. (1995) *From Pram to Primary: Parenting small children from birth to age six or seven*. Newry: Family Caring Trust.

Useful resources

The Magination Press specialises in books that help young children deal with personal or psychological concerns. You can get a catalogue from The Eurospan Group, 3 Henrietta Street, Covent Garden, London WC2E 8LU.

Videos, books and resources from Lucky Duck Publishing Ltd., c/o SAGE Publications Ltd., 1 Oliver's Yard, 55 City Road, London EC1Y 1SP. Website: www.luckyduck.co.uk

The *Understanding Childhood* leaflets available from The Child Psychotherapy Trust, Star House, 104–108 Grafton Road, London NW5 4BD. Website: www.childpsychotherapytrust.org.uk

Organisations and support groups

Barnardo's: provides care and support for children in need and their families, with projects throughout the UK.
Barnardo's, Tanners Lane, Barkingside, Ilford, Essex IG6 1QG
Tel: 020 8550 8822
Website: www.barnardos.org.uk

National Children's Bureau (NCB): a multidisciplinary organisation concerned with the promotion and identification of the interests of all children and young people. Involved in research, policy and practice development, and consultancy.
NCB, 8 Wakley Street, London EC1V 7QE
Tel: 020 7843 6000   Fax: 020 7278 9512
Website: www.ncb.org.uk

National Council of Voluntary Child Care Organisations: umbrella group for voluntary organisations dealing with children. Ensuring the well-being and safeguarding of children and families and maximising the voluntary sector's contribution to the provision of services.
NCVCCO, Unit 4, Pride Court, 80–82 White Lion Street, London N1 9PF
Tel: 020 7833 3319
Website: www.ncvcco.org.uk

National Portage Association: for Portage parents and workers, and for training in Portage which includes the S.T.A.R. approach. Portage is a home-based teaching approach for young children with SEN and their families.
National Portage Association, 127 Monks Dale, Yeovil, Somerset BA21 3JE
Email: info@portage.org.uk
Website: www.portage.org.uk